The AMAZING THING CALLED MEMORY

Written by KELLEY WILLIAMS | Designed by ROBIN FIGHT

You walk through the gate of the picturesque country farm on a crisp fall morning, ready to see all the animals, taste the fresh ice cream and fried apple pies, and maybe even milk a cow. This is your first time on a farm, and you want to remember everything!

The ability to remember things is one of the brain's most important functions. Without memory, you would not know how to eat your breakfast, tie your shoes, or pedal a bike. If you had no memory, you wouldn't even recognize the faces and names of people you see every day or remember anything you learn in school, and you definitely would not remember your day on the farm.

"WITHOUT MEMORY, THERE IS NO CULTURE. WITHOUT MEMORY, THERE WOULD BE NO CIVILIZATION, NO SOCIETY, NO FUTURE."

ELIE WIESEL
WINNER OF THE NOBEL PEACE PRIZE IN 1986

memory

Memory is fascinating, complicated, and crucial to our ability to thrive. To understand how it works, we are going to take a look at the parts of the brain that are involved in memory, the different kinds of memory, why and how we forget things, and some case studies of people with unusual memory abilities and disabilities. Let's dive into this amazing thing called memory!

Study this number for 15 seconds:

235422101

You will be asked to recall it later in the book.

MEMORY: the collection of physical structures and internal processes in the human body that work together to store and retrieve information

Your Worldwide Memory News Source

June 23, 2012

MEMORY NEWS
PRIJESH MERLIN SETS RECORD

On June 23, 2012, **Prijesh Merlin** of India won the record for the most random objects memorized. He was able to recite the names of 470 random objects in the order in which they were read to him.

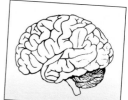

3

BRAIN ANATOMY

Neurons are the cells in your body that pass electrical impulses between each other across a gap called a **synapse**. These impulses are packaged in a chemical called a **neurotransmitter** and move from the end of one neuron, called the **axon**, through the synapse, and into a **dendrite** of the next neuron. In this way, neurons act as messengers from your brain to other parts of your body.

NEURON: the basic unit of the human body's nervous system; carries electrical impulses around the body

SYNAPSE: a tiny junction, across which one neuron passes electrical impulses to another neuron

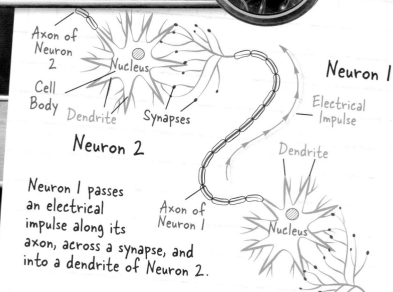

Axon of Neuron 2

Cell Body

Nucleus

Dendrite

Synapses

Neuron 2

Neuron 1

Electrical Impulse

Dendrite

Axon of Neuron 1

Nucleus

Neuron 1 passes an electrical impulse along its axon, across a synapse, and into a dendrite of Neuron 2.

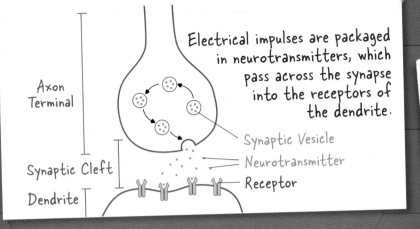

Electrical impulses are packaged in neurotransmitters, which pass across the synapse into the receptors of the dendrite.

Axon Terminal

Synaptic Cleft

Dendrite

Synaptic Vesicle

Neurotransmitter

Receptor

Some electrical impulses move along to a part of the brain called the **hippocampus**. The hippocampus acts as a truck stop, temporarily storing information that the brain wants to be able to retrieve later before shipping it along to be stored in long-term memory. As you process an event, the neurons, synapses, and hippocampus work together to take the input from what is happening around you, turn it into electrical signals, and store those signals as memories.

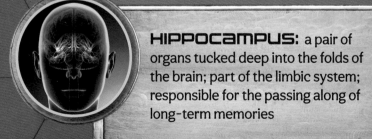

HIPPOCAMPUS: a pair of organs tucked deep into the folds of the brain; part of the limbic system; responsible for the passing along of long-term memories

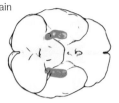

Hippocampus, underside view of brain

CASE STUDY

PATIENT H.M.

In 1953, surgeons removed both sides of **Henry Molaison's** hippocampus in an attempt to stop chronic, debilitating seizures. The surgery worked to stop the seizures, but when Henry woke up, he could no longer form new memories. He remembered a few events from his childhood, historical events, and a few facts about his parents, but he was not able to make or retain new memories. Previous to Henry's surgery, scientists believed that the brain worked as a whole to take in and store memories. However, the discovery that Henry still retained his motor memories, intellect, and personality led the scientists to research the possibility that different parts of the brain were responsible for different kinds of memory.

Let's head back to the farm and see what happens to the information our bodies take in about our environment. As you walk around, your senses are overwhelmed with scents, sounds, and sights. The enticing aroma of deep-fried apple pies wafts on the breeze while the sounds of cows bellowing and children playing in the corn maze reach your ears. You can see and smell the sheep, goats, and alpacas in their pens and hear the snorting of pigs.

sensory memory:
raw environmental data coming in from our senses; stored for just a few milliseconds in the temporal lobe or other parts of the brain

SENSORY MEMORY

Amazingly enough, your brain is able to take in a large amount of sensory data and process it very quickly, although your brain may only pay special attention to certain pieces of information coming in. All that data from what you are seeing, hearing, and smelling at the farm is **encoded**, or turned into electrical signals that your nervous system can use. Neurons carry those signals from your nose, ears, and eyes to be processed in the **temporal lobe**, or the part of the brain that is involved with each specific sense.

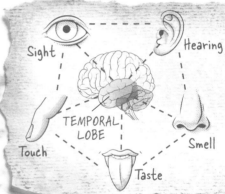

Sight

Hearing

TEMPORAL LOBE

Touch

Smell

Taste

The temporal lobe processes the signals you take in from your five senses (sight, hearing, smell, taste, and touch).

ENCODING: the process by which information coming in through the senses is changed into a form that the brain can use and store

Even though the original event, such as a horse whinnying loudly, has ended, your brain is able to retain, in sharp detail, the memory of that sound just long enough to process it and decide whether to move it along to short-term memory or discard it.

7

SHORT-TERM MEMORY

From the sensory memory stage, some encoded data will move into short-term memory. Information stored here will be remembered longer than sensory memory, but still for only a short time. These memories are things that have just recently happened, such as what you had for breakfast this morning or details from a book you read yesterday. When you learn someone's name for the first time, it is placed in short-term memory and will be forgotten easily if it is not practiced.

Hello
my name is
Adam

SHORT-TERM MEMORY:

- Memories are stored in the prefrontal cortex of the brain.
- Lasts no longer than 30 seconds
- Low capacity
- Most people can hold only between five and seven items in their short-term memory at once.

Do you remember the number you read at the beginning of this book? When you read the number, your eyes took in that information as sensory memory. Then the number seated itself in your short-term memory. If you don't make an effort to practice the number, you might forget it by the end of this book, and most certainly by tomorrow.

Did you remember this number?

235422101

Take a look below at where we are so far on the journey of a memory. The next step for the memory depends on whether or not the brain decides it is important enough to move it into long-term storage.

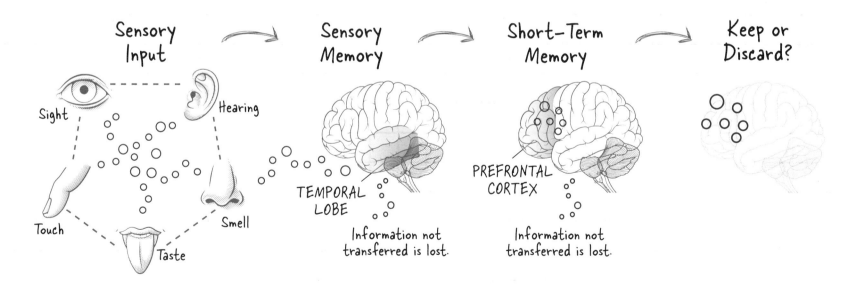

Sensory Input — Sight, Hearing, Touch, Smell, Taste

Sensory Memory — TEMPORAL LOBE — Information not transferred is lost.

Short-Term Memory — PREFRONTAL CORTEX — Information not transferred is lost.

Keep or Discard?

Walking between two aisles of farm animals, you hear a commotion. Some of the pigs have escaped their pen and are running past you, squealing. Shouting farmers are chasing them, and you chase after them to see if you can help. When you think back to the farm years later, you might not remember exactly what you wore or ate, but you will probably remember a lot of details about the great pig escape.

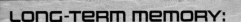

LONG-TERM MEMORY:
the final resting place for a memory the brain has decided to keep; stored in different areas of the brain where there is thought to be unlimited storage capacity, including the temporal lobe, basal ganglia, and parietal and occipital regions

LONG-TERM MEMORY

The memory of the pigs was interesting enough that your brain moved it from your short-term memory to your long-term memory, and your neurons will rehearse the information every time you think about it or retell the story to someone else.

Your Worldwide Memory News Source

MEMORY NEWS

2010

YAN JIASHOU YOUNGEST WINNER OF WORLD MEMORY CHAMPIONSHIP

In 2010, at just 10 years old, **Yan Jiashou** from China became the youngest person to win the World Memory Championship. She broke the tournament record for points earned with feats that included memorizing 646 random sequences of poker cards and 1,080 sequences of numbers in under an hour.

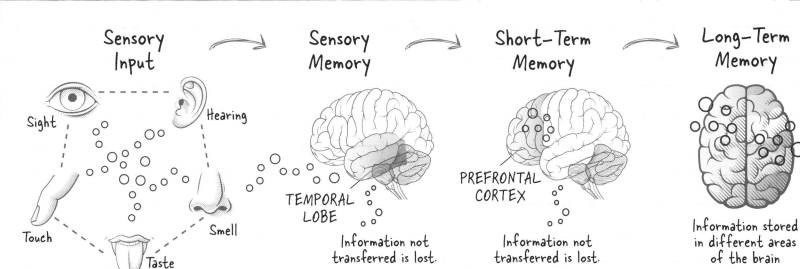

Sensory Input

Sight

Hearing

Touch

Smell

Taste

Sensory Memory

TEMPORAL LOBE

Information not transferred is lost.

Short-Term Memory

PREFRONTAL CORTEX

Information not transferred is lost.

Long-Term Memory

Information stored in different areas of the brain

MORE ON NEURONS & SYNAPSES

You might be wondering what role the neurons and synapses play in transporting and solidifying memories in long-term storage. Just like a muscle, memories that are activated more often strengthen the synapses, while synapses containing memories that aren't recalled or needed as much get weaker and fade over time.

CAN YOU BELIEVE *THIS*?

A man named **Stephen Wiltshire** has a special talent. He once took a brief helicopter ride over New York City. Upon landing, he was able to accurately recreate the whole scene from memory, including the number and placement of windows on the buildings, by drawing it on a 5.8-meter (19-foot) roll of paper.

When a strong memory activates a neuron, it causes a **spike** in that neuron, which releases neurotransmitters from its axon into the synapse between itself and the next neuron. If the memory is to be stored for a long time and recalled easily, the dendritic end of the neuron on the other side of the synapse will have a large concentration of receptors for the neurotransmitters. The more the memory is used, the more neurotransmitters are released and received, and the stronger and longer lasting the memory becomes.

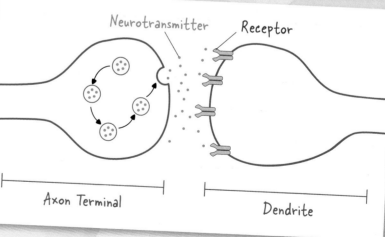

SYNAPTIC PLASTICITY: the ability of a synapse to transmit different strengths of signals between neurons

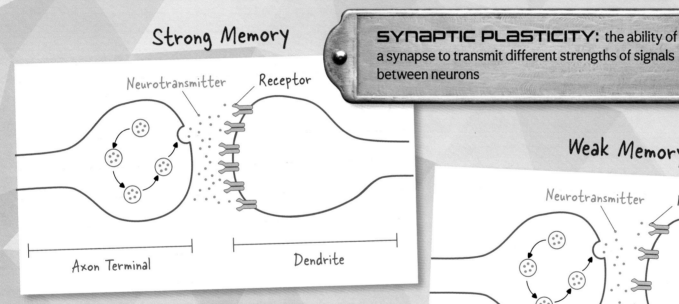

Strong Memory

Neurotransmitter   Receptor

Axon Terminal   Dendrite

Large concentration of neurotransmitters and receptors

Weak Memory

Neurotransmitter   Receptor

Axon Terminal   Dendrite

Fewer neurotransmitters and receptors

TYPES OF LONG-TERM MEMORY

IMPLICIT MEMORY

Implicit memories are your unconscious memory—the things you know how to do without thinking about them. There are many types of implicit memories. Two of them are *procedural learning* and *classical conditioning*.

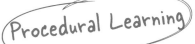

Procedural Learning

- Riding a bike
- Brushing your teeth
- Tying your shoes

Classical Conditioning (Learned Response)

- Fear of falling off the monkey bars because you've fallen off before
- Salivating when you smell your favorite food because you know how good it tastes
- Happiness when you hear holiday music

explicit memory

An explicit memory happens when you intentionally remember something that has happened to you or that you've learned in the past. There are two types of explicit memory: *episodic memory* and *semantic memory*.

Episodic Memory

- The great pig escape
- Walking into your surprise party
- Getting your first car

Semantic Memory (General Knowledge)

- Historical facts
- Birthdays of friends
- Locations of different countries on a map

CASE STUDY

JILL PRICE

Can you imagine having such good long-term memory that you can remember almost everything that has ever happened to you? A woman named **Jill Price** was the first person officially diagnosed with a condition called hyperthymesia, a condition in which a person can remember almost everything that has ever happened to him or her. Jill can remember every detail from every day in her life starting in 1980, when she was 14. In her autobiography, *The Woman Who Can't Forget*, Jill writes, "Give me a date from that year forward and I can instantly tell you what day of the week it was, what I did on that day, and any major event that took place–or even minor events . . . for good or for bad."

A scan of her brain did not show any abnormalities in the hippocampus or other areas associated with memory. Scientists still aren't sure what causes this condition, which has been diagnosed in only about 60 people worldwide as of 2022.

So how do we use the short-term and long-term memories that we have stored in our brains? We retrieve the memories for only a short period of time in an area of memory called **working memory**. Much like a sticky note for our brains, working memory is held temporarily so we can use the information to tackle the tasks that are right before us. Do you remember the number you read at the beginning of the book? As you read the question, your brain is working to pull that number into your working memory so you can recite it correctly.

2 + 2 = ?

WORKING MEMORY

FIRST
you memorize an
addition fact:

2 + 2 = 4

NEXT
the addition fact moves
into your long-term
memory storage.

FINALLY
the addition fact is needed
for a test, so it is moved
into working memory to be
used for a few seconds.

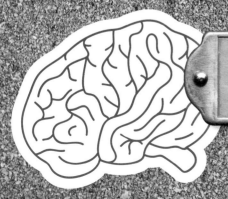

WORKING MEMORY: the place where we
hold temporary memories and information to be used
immediately; processed in the prefrontal cortex of the brain

It's been a year since your trip to the farm, and you're visiting a friend you haven't seen in a long time. The two of you begin to talk about favorite fall activities, and you're reminded of the pig story. To be able to tell your friend the story, you have to retrieve it from your long-term memory. There are three methods of memory retrieval.

1. Memory Recall

Memory recall involves remembering information without being given any clues to help you.

Example: a test with an essay section that requires you to produce the information without anything to help you remember the answer

2. Memory Recognition

Memory recognition is remembering information because you are given clues to help.

Example: the multiple-choice section of a test that requires you to simply recognize the correct answer already shown

MEMORY RETRIEVAL

MEMORY RETRIEVAL:

Memory retrieval happens when we remember information that has been encoded and stored in our brains in the past. Usually, the same area in our brains is activated that was used when we formed the memory in the first place.

Communications: Early Bird receives and sends telephone calls and TV programs between the U.S. and Europe.

Navigation: Transit satellites guide ships, planes, and submarines located anywhere around the world.

3. Memory Relearning

When you remind yourself of information you used to know, this is memory relearning.

Example: failing the test and having to study the information again, or "refreshing your memory"

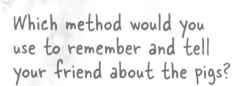

Which method would you use to remember and tell your friend about the pigs?

MEMORY TRICKS

Speaking of studying for tests, there are several tricks you can use to help you remember information you have learned. The depth of attention you pay to something the first time has an effect on how strong the memory becomes. Let's take that number you saw on the first page of the book. Can you remember it? One theory about how well we remember things we've learned has to do with how we attach meaning to, or process, the memory.

SHALLOW PROCESSING

If you had simply repeated the number to yourself a few times and noticed something like what the font looked like or how big or small the numbers were, you might have had a chance of remembering it by this point in the book. This is **shallow processing**, and it usually results in only short-term retention of the information.

DEEP PROCESSING

A better way to remember a piece of information is to attach a deeper meaning to it in a method called **deep processing**. The following **mnemonic devices** would have helped you remember the number.

You could have **chunked**, or divided, the numbers into smaller sets that were easier to remember, like this phony phone number:
235-422-101

Maybe you **associated** the number with someone's birthday or a date that is special to you, like these:
2/3/54; 2/21/01

Or possibly you were able to associate the numbers with some mathematical equations like these:
$2 + 3 = 5; 4 - 2 = 2; 1 + 0 = 1$

MNEMONIC DEVICES: methods of organizing information to make it easier to remember; for example, using the acronym ROY G. BIV to remember the colors of the rainbow (red, orange, yellow, green, blue, indigo, violet)

Have you ever been frustrated that you couldn't remember something important, such as where you put the television remote control last week? That's okay because a normal level of forgetting is actually good for our brains! It helps us clear out useless information to make room for important memories and new learning. Forgetting helps our brains be more efficient and make better decisions. Forgetting is a way to "tune out the noise."

Decay

When memories aren't used often, the synapses weaken, and the memory fades over time. Your memory of the people you saw at the farm will fade quickly because they weren't already familiar to you.

Interference

New memories constantly interfere with and override old memories. If you go to the farm again next year, your memory of that excursion might override your memory of this year's trip, and you could forget many of the details from this trip.

FORGETTING

The brain uses sleep to tidy up the multiple memories it has stored throughout the day. Recent research in mice suggests that the synapses for some memories reset and may even shrink while we sleep. This makes room for more information to be taken in the next day. During the night after your day at the farm, your brain will probably strengthen the synapses that hold the memory of the pigs escaping but weaken the synapses that hold information about the minor details of the day.

False Memories

A false memory of an event is similar to, but not exactly the same as, forgetting. When memories transfer from short-term to long-term memory, some bits and pieces can get lost in the movement. Then your brain might fill in details that aren't actually true. After a few weeks or months, you and a friend might disagree about the order in which you saw the animals at the farm.

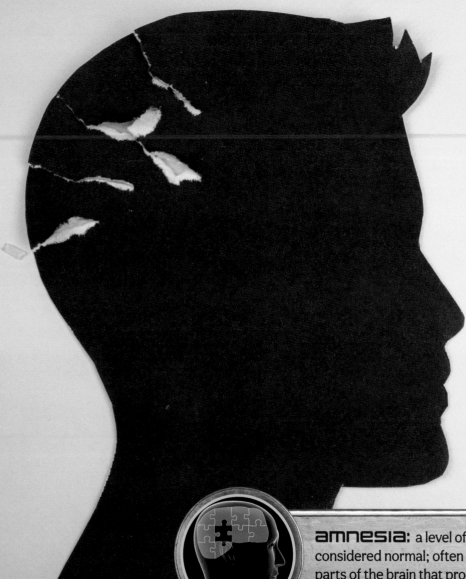

amnesia

Everyone experiences normal forgetting, but there are extreme cases of memory loss that affect some people. Amnesia is a fascinating condition that can have severe and long-lasting effects on people's lives.

TYPES OF amnesia

Retrograde: cannot recall events that happened before the onset of amnesia

Anterograde: cannot form new memories of events that happen after the onset of amnesia

Infantile: cannot recall events from early childhood

amnesia: a level of memory loss beyond what's considered normal; often caused by damage to the parts of the brain that process memories

Amnesia usually does not affect a person's personality, intellect, identity, or ability to perform simple physical tasks, such as walking or eating.

causes of amnesia

Injury or illness: an illness that affects the brain, or a physical injury to the head, which may cause either retrograde or anterograde amnesia

Emotional trauma: when the brain blocks the memories from a traumatic event

Dementia: severe memory loss that can be caused by aging

CASE STUDY
CLIVE WEARING

Struck by a rare brain infection at the age of 47, former musician **Clive Wearing** immediately began to suffer from the worst known case of total amnesia in the world. The disease damaged his hippocampus, causing him to forget anything that happened before a thirty-second window. He was no longer able to remember anything from his past (retrograde amnesia) or make new memories (anterograde amnesia). Every few seconds, everything seemed brand new to him. Clive was once found repeatedly opening and closing his hand over a piece of chocolate, exclaiming, "Look! It's new!" each time he opened his hand again. As of 2022, Clive still lives in a long-term care facility in a constant state of believing he has just awakened from being dead or in a coma.

memory and aging

All parts of our bodies weaken as we get older, and the brain is no exception. The hippocampus, neurons, synapses, and cortex areas shrink and lose some blood flow just as the rest of the body does, and this affects memory. Starting as early as age 45, we begin to lose our mental sharpness, abilities to learn new information, and abilities to retain and recall memories.

Keep your brain fit and sharp!

- Learn a new language.
- Learn how to play a musical instrument.
- Exercise regularly.
- Eat a healthy diet.
- Get enough sleep.
- Play brain games and do puzzles.

CAREER STUDY

FAMOUS COGNITIVE NEUROSCIENTISTS

1890s

IVAN PAVLOV: A Russian scientist who used dogs as subjects to study their responses to food by salivating, Pavlov discovered the concept of classical conditioning and helped create methods to study memory and behavior in people.

Ivan Pavlov

1950

KARL LASHLEY: By experimenting on rats, Lashley strove to understand the connection between the processes of memory and learning and the physical structures of the brain. He helped prove that memories are not constrained to a single spot in the brain and that damage to part of the brain can affect memory.

1970

ERIC KANDEL: Awarded the Nobel Prize in Physiology or Medicine in 2000, Kandel studied marine snails to discover that learning new things caused the chemical signals to change the structure of the synapses between cells. This led to the theory that short-term and long-term memories are formed by different signals.

Eric Kandel

1970s–1990s

ELIZABETH LOFTUS: Loftus did extensive research on the concept of false memories, especially pertaining to people testifying in court cases. In one study, she showed subjects a video of a crime and then a news report with incorrect information about the crime. When asked about the details of the crime, people tended to mix up what they'd seen on the video and what they'd heard on the news report.

amazing facts about memory

DÉJÀ VU

If you've ever had the sudden feeling that you've been in a place or experienced something before when you actually haven't, that's a phenomenon called *déjà vu*. Scientists aren't sure why this happens to about 60% of people.

THE POWER OF SCENT

More than any of our other senses, the memories of certain smells connected to emotional events are resistant to decay and interference. This is called olfactory memory, and you've probably experienced it before!

THE DOORWAY EFFECT

Have you ever watched someone walk into a room,
look confused, and walk back out? That person might
have been experiencing what psychologists call the
"doorway effect." It is believed that walking through
a doorway causes a reset of working memory, which
makes it easy for a person to walk into a room intending
to get or do something and forget what he or she was
there for as soon as he or she crosses the doorway.

Where would you be without your memory? From something as simple as knowing how to talk, walk, or bring your spoon to your mouth to remembering complicated math formulas and what you had for dinner last week, memory is an essential part of your brain's functions.

Thanks to the study of neuroscience, we know much more about how memory works, how illnesses and injuries might affect memory, how to strengthen our memory skills, and how to keep our brains as healthy as possible for as long as possible. As you go about your day, stop and appreciate how hard your brain is working to encode, store, and retrieve those important memories.

"TIME MOVES IN ONE DIRECTION, MEMORY IN ANOTHER."

WILLIAM GIBSON

AMERICAN-CANADIAN AUTHOR AND ESSAYIST

CONCLUSION